God's Debt-Free Guarantee

by

John Avanzini

Harrison House
Tulsa, Oklahoma

Copyright © 1994 by International Faith Center, Inc., P.O. Box 917001, Fort Worth, Texas 76117-9001.
Printed in the United States of America.
All rights reserved under International Copyright Law. Contents and/or cover may not be reproduced in whole or in part in any form without the express written consent of the publisher.

God's Debt-Free Guarantee

ISBN: 0-892-74-919-9

First Printing: 175,000 copies

Unless otherwise indicated, all Scripture quotations are taken from the *King James Version* of the Bible.

Verses marked **Amplified** are Scripture taken from THE AMPLIFIED BIBLE, Old Testament copyright © 1965, 1987 by The Zondervan Corporation. The Amplified New Testament copyright © 1958, 1987 by The Lockman Foundation. Used by permission.

For emphasis, the author has placed selected words from the Bible quotations in italics.

Testimonies have been grammatically corrected and edited slightly.

Harrison House
P.O. Box 35035
Tulsa, OK 74153

This book is respectfully dedicated

to the memory of

Rev. John Boden

a faithful friend and partner in this ministry.

While our friendship was short,

the memory of it will last forever.

Contents

1. God's Debt-Free Guarantee 9

2. Three Things You Must Know 17

3. Things to Do 35

4. An Open Heaven 49

5. An Out-of-Debt Flow 61

6. Putting Heaven on Notice 69

7. Your Goliath Must Fall 81

   My Declaration of Acceptance
of God's Debt-Free Guarantee 91

1

God's Debt-Free Guarantee

... the king ... will ... make his father's
house free in Israel.
1 Samuel 17:25

Few people realize how big the reward David received for killing Goliath really was. The Word of God tells us that besides winning two other valuable prizes, the king cancelled *every single debt David's father owed* or ever would owe.

Just think about it for a moment. By simply allowing God to use him, a little shepherd boy received a *debt-free guarantee* from the highest authority in his nation. Keep in mind that David was a part of his father's house in the same way that David's children would be a part of David's household. Therefore, when David brought an end to Goliath's reign of terror, he brought an end to the bondage of debt over not only his father's life, but his own life as well.

An Extensive Guarantee

Notice that David's debt-free guarantee was powerful because the word of the king backed it up. Let's take a closer look at Scripture and see exactly what the king promised to do for the person who would slay the giant called "Goliath."

> **. . . Have ye seen this man that is come up? surely to defy Israel is he come up: and it shall be, that the man who killeth him, the king will enrich him with great riches, and will give him his daughter,** *and make his father's house free in Israel.*
>
> **1 Samuel 17:25**

Scripture tells us there would be three rewards for the person who killed the giant. First of all, the king would give the overcomer great financial riches. He would also allow him to marry his daughter. These two rewards meant the overcomer would live like a king. Beyond that, he would receive a prize that would change everything for his father's family. The entire family of the giant-slayer would live the rest of their lives *totally free from the bondage of debt.* This is the part of the promise I would like to focus your attention on in this book. I want to show you, step by step, how to lay hold on God's debt-free guarantee and put it to work in your life.

Stripped Naked

Let me now draw your attention to another important piece of information this portion of Scripture gives us. I want you to see the literal meaning of the name *Goliath.* There is much more to this name than meets the eye.

Upon close examination, you will find that *Goliath* is not a Philistine name. Instead, it is a name the Hebrews gave to the giant. *Strong's Concordance* lists it as the Hebrew word #1555. There the spelling is only slightly different from our English spelling. Instead of using an "i," the Hebrew word contains a "y." Goliath comes from word

#1540, *galah,* which the Hebrew dictionary defines as meaning "to denude" or "to make nude."

When it describes the giant Goliath, the literal meaning of the word is *"the one who takes captives and strips them naked."* This definition is significant because *Goliath* is a descriptive name the Hebrews had given to the giant. It explains how the Hebrews found themselves after they had come under his control. He had taken them captive, and then stripped them naked!

Debt Will Strip You

If you think about it a moment, you will have to conclude that the name *Goliath* perfectly describes how the spirit of debt affects its victims. After working hard for your money, then finding that federal withholding taxes have stripped away 25 to 35 percent of your hard-earned pay, does anything describe the feeling more perfectly than being stripped? This feeling doesn't get any better when you realize the taxes you pay are the direct result of a free-spending, debt-hungry legislature that has overspent and borrowed to cover it up for longer than anyone can remember.

As if your taxes aren't enough, then comes the added discouragement of seeing your house payment, car payment, credit-card debt, second mortgages, and other bills systematically strip away the remainder of your paycheck!

Anyone who has been in debt for any length of time at all will quickly tell you how it feels. It is as if you have been taken captive and systematically stripped naked.

You can describe debt as a horrible, ripping sensation, one that never stops tearing away at your hopes and dreams.

Dear friend, if you are in debt, you had better pay close attention to the things the Spirit of God has to say to you in this book. There is only one thing that will stop the devastation debt is bringing into your life. You must *totally defeat the goliath of debt* that has come to feed on your dreams.

Debt is a spirit. It's a ruling spirit whose only purpose is to turn you into a servant. Please don't think I have made this conclusion on my own. It is a truth that comes from the Word of God, for if you are a borrower, the Bible says you have become a servant.

> ... the borrower is servant to the lender.
> Proverbs 22:7

Five Powerful Concepts

The biblical account of David's victory over the giant contains special truth that will help you to lay a firm hold on God's debt-free guarantee. The Word of God tells us when he stepped onto the battlefield to face Goliath, David brought something special with him. In his hand he had five smooth stones. He would use them as ammunition against Goliath. Scripture tells us he took these stones out of the brook.

> **And he took ... five smooth stones out of the brook. ...**
> **1 Samuel 17:40**

Water is often a type of the Holy Scriptures.

**That he might sanctify and cleanse it with
the washing of** *water by the word.*
Ephesians 5:26

Without having to use much imagination, you can easily see the brook as representing the Word of God.

Please notice something important about the stones David took from the brook. They were smooth stones. Their condition tells us they had been in the brook for a very long time. The continuous flow of the water over them had worn away all the rough edges. This is the way it is with all the truth that comes from the Word of God. Everything you find in the Bible is tried and true and has withstood the test of time.

. . . thy word is truth.
John 17:17

Illustrations from the Bible have worked as inspiration for others throughout the ages, and this one will start working for you today. I am going to show you how to use five proven concepts from the Bible to win your battle with the Goliath of debt you now face. These truths carry with them a promise of God's power to help you in your war on debt.

The Debt-Free Guarantee

Any one of the stones I am about to place in your hand has enough power in it to remove forever the debt you are now facing. However, when you put them all together and faithfully operate them, they will go beyond just getting you out of debt. They will bring you into God's debt-free guarantee.

13

Now please don't look upon these concepts as if they were my own ideas. Instead, I want you to see them for what they really are. They are *God's ideas*. The further you read in this book, the more obvious it will become that they could not be the thoughts of a mere man. They are the thoughts of our great God.

High-Powered Truth Awaits You

The five powerful concepts I will put at your disposal are as follows:

Stone #1: Three things you must know!

First, your God is a debt-cancelling God. *Second,* He is no respecter of persons. *Third,* He wants you out of debt.

Stone #2: Two things you must start doing!

First, you must start doing the things that will get you out of debt. *Second,* you must start speaking as if you are going to be debt free.

Stone #3: Create an open heaven!

You must be a faithful tither.

Stone #4: Create an out-of-debt flow!

You must use the golden rule in your war on debt.

Stone #5: Place heaven on notice!

You must build a memorial that declares your intention to be debt free.

Keep your spirit open, because the pages of this book are filled with divine revelation that will place within your grasp God's debt-free guarantee.

The Big Mistake

Please don't make the mistake of thinking that by faithfully making your payments each month, you will one day get out of debt. It just doesn't work that way. If it did, you would constantly be hearing about people who were becoming debt free. I say this because the vast majority of the people who are in debt, faithfully pay their bills each month. However, few of them ever get out of debt. The reason for this situation is simple. The spirit of debt keeps dragging them in deeper and deeper.

If you ever hope to overcome the spirit of debt, *you must have a plan.* It must be a powerful plan, one that uses the very force of God to guarantee your victory.

After faithfully studying about debt for the past fifteen years, I can honestly say nothing is more effective in setting people permanently free from it than the truth in God's Word. However, you must remember it is not just the truth that sets you free. It is the truth of God's Word that *you know.* Believe me, as long as you don't know a truth, you cannot walk in it.

> . . . ye shall *know* the truth, and the truth
> *[you know]* shall make you free.
> John 8:32

Now please don't look upon God's debt-free guarantee as a new idea, for it is not. It is simply a *neglected truth.*

You Can Defeat Goliath

Thank God for His wonderful Word! In it He tells us how to overcome anything and everything the devil can possibly use against us.

> ... they [people just like you] overcame him
> [the devil] ... by the word of their testimony. ...
> **Revelation 12:11**

The Apostle John tells us overcoming power comes to us from the testimonies of other believers. Yes, you are reading correctly. God has given the victory testimonies of others the ability to impart to you the inner strength and insight you need to overcome the devil. Throughout this book I will be sharing testimonies from people just like you who have defeated the Goliath of debt. Their victory reports will help increase your faith as you begin your out-of-debt program.

If you will now open your hand and turn the page, I will drop stone #1 into it.

2

Three Things You Must Know

. . . the truth [you know] shall make you
free.

John 8:32

God is definitely not silent on the subject of debt. The Bible gives instance after instance in which God miraculously cancels the debts of His people. In fact, the Holy Bible has more to say about the cancellation of people's debts than it does about blind eyes being opened, or lame legs walking. The Word of God actually speaks of debt cancellation from cover to cover.

Stone #1

This first stone you must lay hold of is an *information stone*. God has three important pieces of information you must firmly fix in your mind. It is important that you thoroughly understand each of these principles. As soon as you do, you will immediately begin to feel the energy of God flowing into your out-of-debt program. Please believe me. These are not just idle words. Real, *enabling power will flow from God's life into your life.*

I hope you are aware that power does flow from God to man. There are a number of scriptural references that prove this fact. If you remember, God's power flowed when the woman with the issue of blood touched the hem of our Lord's garment. As soon as she touched the truth

(Jesus), power flowed from Him, to her. It was the kind of power she needed, for it instantly healed her body, stopping her flow of blood.

> . . . Jesus, immediately *knowing in himself that virtue had gone out of him,* turned him about in the press, and said, Who touched my clothes?
> **Mark 5:30**

In that same way, the power you need will flow from God directly into your life. Each of these truths from God's Word will release a burst of divine power into your out-of-debt program.

The three truths you must know are as follows:

1. God is a debt-cancelling God.

2. God is no respecter of persons.

3. God wants you to be debt free.

God Can Do Anything

It goes without saying that God can do anything. The Bible clearly states He can.

> . . . Lord God . . . there is nothing too hard for thee.
> **Jeremiah 32:17**

There can be no question about it. Jehovah God can cancel debt. With this truth stated, let me go on to say that simply knowing God *can* cancel debt will not release any significant amount of God's power into your out-of-debt program. Let me explain what I mean by the following illustration.

Let's say you needed $100,000 to buy a house. It goes without saying, God is capable of causing a plant in your garden miraculously to grow thousand-dollar bills instead of leaves. He could allow a hundred of these thousand-dollar bills to grow on your miraculous money tree. This money would amount to the $100,000 you desired for the purchase of the house.

No one in his right mind would dare say this miracle would be impossible for God to perform, especially when you know He has done stranger things before. In fact, He has caused a donkey to speak (Numbers 22:28), an ax head to swim (2 Kings 6:6), and oil to multiply (2 Kings 4:5,6). However, *knowing God is able* to do a thing *does not mean He will* do it.

God Has Cancelled Debt Before

The first piece of information you must know is *not* that God is *capable* of cancelling debt. You must know *He has cancelled debt before.* Let me now take you through the Word of God and show you some of the many miraculous debt cancellations God has performed in the past.

A Widow's Debt Is Cancelled (2 Kings 4:1-7)

God supernaturally intervened and cancelled a widow's debt. He did it the same day her two sons were to become servants of the lender. You will find the account of this miracle of debt cancellation in the fourth chapter of 2 Kings. The Scripture tells us the poor woman's husband had died. While Scripture doesn't specifically give the cause of his death, it could well have been the pressure that debt brought to bear upon his life. Scripture goes on to tell us her two sons would have to spend many years at hard labor paying off their daddy's debt.

In a desperate, last-minute attempt, the widow turns to her man of God for help with her financial problem just moments before it would be too late. As soon as she tells him of her circumstances, he speaks a powerful word of deliverance to her. He tells her she must borrow vessels, many vessels. She must then go into her house and begin to pour her meager supply of oil into the vessels she has borrowed.

As soon as she obeys the prophet, *her miraculous debt cancellation begins to materialize.* It is such a powerful miracle that it makes her and her two sons totally debt free and financially set for life. Her little pot of oil miraculously multiplies into many gallons of oil.

Listen as her man of God tells her to sell the oil, pay her debt, and use the surplus for retirement.

> **. . . Go, sell the oil, and pay thy debt, and**
> **live thou and thy children of the rest.**
> **2 Kings 4:7**

Carefully notice that the day the devil intended to be her worst, God turned into *her best.* All of this activity took place because she knew her God was a debt-cancelling God. When she turned to Jehovah God for help with her debt instead of turning to the lender, she released the power of God into her out-of-debt program. She did not have to face the evil day alone. She took her debt problem to God in faith, believing He was a debt-cancelling God.

Her belief paid off when her debt-cancelling miracle became a reality.

I want you to say the following sentence out loud. *"My God is a debt-cancelling God!"*

Testimony:
We have had a miraculous debt cancellation of $6,000 on one of our credit cards. *T. & M.O.—Clarkston, GA*

A Borrowed Ax Head Swims (2 Kings 6:5-7)

Just a few pages further in the Book of 2 Kings, we find yet another miraculous debt cancellation. It takes place in the life of a young man who has lost an ax head in the river. The thing that makes the loss of the ax head so important is that it was not just any old ax head. Scripture tells us it was a borrowed ax head.

> **. . . Alas, master! for it was borrowed.**
> **2 Kings 6:5**

Notice the first thing the young man does. He calls out for help from God. It would seem as if he should call for the best diver, or maybe the best swimmer. However, he doesn't. Instead he calls on God. His action leads us to believe he knew his God was a debt-cancelling God.

Please notice that the prophet also believes God to be a debt-cancelling God. As soon as he hears that it was a borrowed ax head, the man of God moves into action, and *the ax head miraculously swims to the surface.*

> . . . and the iron [ax head] did swim.
> . . . And he put out his hand, and took it.
> **2 Kings 6:6,7**

Don't you just know this young man went home rejoicing that his God cancels debt? Think of it. A miracle from God set him free of the pending debt. The same Jehovah God who caused the borrowed ax head to swim up from the bottom of the river is also your God, and He is a debt-cancelling God.

Please say it out loud again. *"My God is a debt-cancelling God!"*

A Nation Becomes Debt Free (Nehemiah 5:1-12)

In the days of Nehemiah, debt had risen to unbelievable levels. It was a day much like our day. The nation was deep in debt. People were borrowing because of the severe problems they were facing.

> . . . We have mortgaged our lands,
> vineyards, and houses, that we might buy corn,
> because of the dearth.
> **Nehemiah 5:3**

Not only that, but they were also borrowing money to pay their taxes.

> . . . We have borrowed money for the king's
> tribute, and that upon our lands and vineyards.
> **Nehemiah 5:4**

This same thing is happening right now in our nation. Many are having to borrow to pay the IRS. However, as grim as all this lack seems, it is but a small problem for our God.

Nehemiah moves in full confidence that the God of Israel is a debt-cancelling God. He commands the lenders to cancel the people's debts and set them free. Miraculously, God leads all the lenders to forgive the whole nation of their debts. Yes, you are reading right. Every one of God's children becomes *debt free in a single day.*

> . . . I [Nehemiah] pray you [the lenders], let us leave off this usury.
>
> Restore, I pray you, to them, even this day, their lands, their vineyards, their oliveyards, and their houses, also the hundredth part of the money, and of the corn, the wine, and the oil, that ye exact of them.
>
> Then said they, We will restore them, and will require nothing of them; so will we do as thou sayest. . . .
>
> **Nehemiah 5:10-12**

Notice that Nehemiah boldly spoke to the people's mountain of debt, and just as surely as he spoke, his faith removed the mountain of debt from his people.

> . . . If ye have faith, and doubt not . . . ye shall *say unto this mountain*, Be thou removed, and be thou cast into the sea; it shall be done.
>
> **Matthew 21:21**

The Bible tells us Nehemiah's people became debt free when they believed in their debt-cancelling God's ability to deliver them.

Let's say it out loud again. *"My God is a debt-cancelling God!"*

Testimony:
   The Lord blessed us with $5,800 to pay off three credit cards. *J.G.—Hollywood, FL*

Jesus Has a Debt Cancelled (Matthew 17:24-27)

The next illustration of God's debt-cancelling power comes from the New Testament. The debt we will now see cancelled is a tax bill. A large number of God's children face delinquent taxes. Many of them write me and ask if God cancels tax bills. Praise God, He most surely does. Better than that, He most surely has.

Scripture tells us that God cancelled a tax bill for someone whom we all know and love. He did it for our Lord and Savior Jesus Christ! The account of this miraculous debt cancellation is in the seventeenth chapter of Matthew. There we find the tax collector confronting Simon Peter. The tax collector asks him if Jesus is going to pay His taxes (tribute money). Simon Peter immediately tells the man that Jesus most certainly is. As Peter leaves the tax collector to get the necessary cash from the treasury, our Lord sets in motion a miracle of debt cancellation that *pays off both of their tax bills.*

Notice that Jesus deliberately prevents Simon from proceeding with his plan to use the cash reserves of the ministry to pay the bill.

> . . . And when he was come into the house, *Jesus prevented him.* . . .
> **Matthew 17:25**

Instead, Jesus sends Simon on a fishing trip. Now please notice it is a special trip, for it is for a single fish. Oh, what a *miraculous fish* it would be, for it would have money in its mouth.

> . . . go thou to the sea, and cast an hook, and take up the fish that first cometh up; and *when thou hast opened his mouth, thou shalt find a piece of money:* that take, and give unto them for me and thee.
>
> **Matthew 17:27**

There it is in black and white. God performed a miracle of debt cancellation for Jesus. Go ahead and say it out loud again, but this time, say it as if you really mean it. *"My God really is a debt-cancelling God!"*

Testimony:
God miraculously paid off our IRS bill and gave us money to sow. *B.B.—Euless, TX*

Biblical Debt Cancellations Abound

You will find many other miraculous debt cancellations throughout God's Word. The following four instances will further help to establish this truth in your heart and mind. Your God goes well beyond just being *able* to cancel debt. He is, in fact, the God who cancels the debts of His people time and time again.

For your further information, see these biblical accounts:

1. A slave named Onesimus was set free from debt (Philemon 10-19).

2. King David's father also became debt free (1 Samuel 17:25).

3. The entire nation of Israel had all of their debts cancelled every seven years. This debt cancellation took place at the time we call the "year of release" (Deuteronomy 15:1,2).

4. At the end of each fifty-year period, Israel had a special debt-cancellation party. It was called the "jubilee." At that time, creditors cancelled all debts and returned all properties to the original owners (Leviticus 25).

I want you to say it one more time. *"My God is a debt-cancelling God!"*

Feel the Power Begin to Flow

Now that you know God has cancelled debt before, I want you to add to this knowledge that *He is the same today as He was yesterday, and He will be the same forever.* With this powerful combination of truth, you will begin immediately to experience the energy of God flowing into your out-of-debt program.

Jesus Christ the same yesterday, and to day, and for ever.
Hebrews 13:8

This is energy-releasing knowledge, for if God has cancelled debt before, the Bible says He will do it again. Hallelujah! Your God is still cancelling debt today. If He did it before, you can depend upon His doing it again.

God Is No Respecter of Persons

There is a second thing you must know. *Your God is no respecter of persons.*

> . . . Of a truth I perceive that God is no respecter of persons.
> **Acts 10:34**

You just learned that God has cancelled debt before. If you add to that knowledge the fact that God is no respecter of persons, you will be able to draw even more of God's power into your out-of-debt program. If you know God has done something special for a specific individual, you can be assured He will do the same thing for you.

He cancelled the debt of the widow (2 Kings 4); He cancelled the debt of the young man who had borrowed the ax head (2 Kings 6); He cancelled the debt of everyone who was with Nehemiah (Nehemiah 5). He even cancelled the debt of our Lord and Savior Jesus Christ (Matthew 17). If you know He helped these folks by cancelling their debts, you can be confident He will be willing to help you with your debts. If He did it for others, *He will do it for you,* because He is not a respecter of persons!

> . . . God is no respecter of persons.
> **Acts 10:34**

God Wants You to Be Debt Free

There is a third thing you must know. When you have learned it, this knowledge will release even more of God's enabling power into your debt-free program. You must know beyond any shadow of a doubt that *God wants you to be debt free.*

Notice I did not say, you must know God doesn't want people to be in debt. You must have personal knowledge that goes beyond this fact if you want even more of God's power in your out-of-debt program. You must know it is God's perfect will for *your life* that you be totally debt free.

Try this information on for size by saying your name in the following sentence. "God wants (your first name) (your last name) to be debt free!" Repeat this sentence as many times as it takes to fill your consciousness with it.

Testimony:
   Through your teaching we realized that God wanted us debt free. At that time we could barely make ends meet, but we declared war on debt, and within a few months we were able to pay off over $6,000 of our debts. *C.D.— Adair, OK*

How God Feels About Your Debt

Just imagine what would happen if you were to stand before God today and ask Him how He feels about your debt, I mean all of it — your house payment, car note, credit cards, as well as all the rest of your unpaid bills. What would His reply be? Would He say, "I really don't pay any attention to your debts. Just use wisdom and don't overload yourself"? Or would He say, "Precious child, *my perfect will for you is that you be totally debt free"?*

God's Word tells you in black and white that He wants you to be debt free. Please take the time to read the first fourteen verses of the twenty-eighth chapter of Deuteronomy. In them you will find that your God says His children who obey Him will be *blessed* people. He says He will actually send the blessings out *to overtake* His obedient children. He promises to bless them in the city, as well as in the field (Deuteronomy 28:3). He says their cupboards will be full. He even says the obedient ones will have savings accounts.

> **Blessed shall be thy basket and thy store [savings].**
> **Deuteronomy 28:5**

He also promises this group they will have plenty of nice things.

> **. . . the Lord shall make thee plenteous in goods. . . .**
> **Deuteronomy 28:11**

The ones who please Him will be ". . . the head and not the tail. . ." (Deuteronomy 28:13).

Now get the rest of this passage! The obedient saints will be debt free!

> **. . . thou shalt lend . . . and *thou shalt not borrow.***
> **Deuteronomy 28:12**

Disobedient Saints Will Walk in Debt

In verse 15 of this same chapter, the writer makes an abrupt turnaround. He speaks to the disobedient saints, the ones who will not walk in His ways. He tells them they will walk in curses instead of blessings.

> But it shall come to pass, if thou wilt not hearken unto the voice of the Lord thy God, to observe to do all his commandments and his statutes which I command thee this day; that all these curses shall come upon thee, and overtake thee.
>
> Deuteronomy 28:15

The list of curses goes on for fifty-three verses. Among them, one thing really stands out. Those who walk contrary to God's will, *walk in debt.*

> The stranger that is within thee shall get up above thee very high; and thou shalt come down very low.
>
> *He shall lend to thee,* and thou shalt not lend to him: *he shall be the head,* and *thou shalt be the tail.*
>
> Deuteronomy 28:43,44

With this information you know God wants you to be debt free. When you have *a specific word* from God, you also have His assurance that you can fulfill it. He promises that His Word will empower you to accomplish His will.

> For with God nothing is ever impossible and *no word from God shall be without power* or impossible of fulfillment.
>
> Luke 1:37, Amplified

The very Word of God that brings you His will for your life, is filled with power to accomplish it. Just think about it. The power to carry out a word from God is always resident in that Word. In other words, God will never speak a word to you that He is not willing to empower you to fulfill. Every word He speaks to you has His power in it to help you accomplish it.

The same Word of God that tells you He wants you to be debt free, carries with it an infusion of God's power that will enable you to overcome the debt you face.

Stone #1 Is Now in Your Hand

I hope you are seeing what a powerful advantage these three pieces of knowledge are giving you. When you know these three facts about God's mind on debt, stone #1 will be in your arsenal. This stone will be ready to deliver God's knock-out punch to the Goliath of debt that holds you captive. The Word of God says that with each of these strategic pieces of knowledge, supernatural power comes to you from God. His power will energize your debt-free program and give it the staying power you will need to rid yourself thoroughly of the spirit of debt. It will become one of the five great weapons that will deliver God's debt-free guarantee to you.

Testimony:
I became aware of the reality of cancelled debt when I called the hospital to get the balance of our account after the birth of our second child and was told we had no balance. *B.G.—Mt. Pleasant, SC*

Energizing Truth

Remember, stone #1 consists of three important truths:

Truth 1: Your God is a debt-cancelling God. If He did it before, He will do it again.

> **Jesus Christ the same yesterday, and to day, and for ever.**
> **Hebrews 13:8**

Knowing this truth releases the power of God to you because *it gives you the knowledge that miraculous debt cancellation is still happening today.*

Truth 2: Your God is no respecter of persons. You now know He has cancelled the debts of other individuals. Therefore, He is willing to do the same for you.

> **... God is no respecter of persons.**
> **Acts 10:34**

Knowing this truth releases God's power to you because *it lets you know that it can also happen to you.*

Truth 3: It is God's will that you be totally debt free.

> **And all these blessings shall come on thee, and overtake thee, if thou shalt hearken unto the voice of the Lord thy God.**
> **... and thou shalt lend ... and thou shalt not borrow.**
> **Deuteronomy 28:2,12**

Knowing this truth releases even more of God's power to you because *you now have a specific word from God* about being debt free. His Word says He wants you out of debt, and *with His word comes the promise* of the power necessary to accomplish it.

> For with God nothing is ever impossible
> and no word from God shall be without power or
> impossible of fulfillment.
>
> Luke 1:37, Amplified

You must now get ready for the release of even more of God's power into your life, for the truth of the next chapter will be equally effective in your out-of-debt program.

3

Things to Do

> . . . faith, if it hath not works, is dead, being alone.
>
> James 2:17

The city where I grew up was unique in many ways. One of them was the colorful sayings the people used to express themselves. They were part of the rich, southern Texas heritage that so greatly influenced my early years. One of those sayings was especially descriptive. It was short and to the point, as well as true! It went like this, *"Talk is cheap."* When someone used this phrase, everyone understood it would take more than talk to get the job done. This statement agrees with the Bible, for it says:

> . . . faith without works is dead.
>
> James 2:20

Nowhere is this saying more true than when it comes to getting out of debt, for unless you take decisive action, absolutely nothing will come of your out-of-debt plan.

Stone #2

The second stone I want to place in your hand will call for some definite *activity on your part*. To receive the full benefit of the divine energy it brings to your out-of-debt program, you are going to have to start doing some things. Simply said, you are going to have to do the things people who are getting out of debt do.

Testimony:
   I got completely out of debt by following your instructions. *K.B.—Toronto, Ontario*

Hearers and Not Doers

I have always been amazed at the number of Christians who choose to only hear the Word, and never seem to do the things it says. I find this situation to be a particular problem when it comes to becoming debt free. Every time I speak to a group about getting out of debt, they give me their undivided attention. After each session, they storm the book table and purchase everything I have available on the subject. However, on my return trip, I find that most of the people who had listened so intently just a short time before, have *made absolutely no attempt* to put into practice any of the principles I taught them. It goes without saying they were eager hearers. Why, they even loaded up with the support material from the book table. However, they just never took the next step and became doers of the words they heard. The Apostle James is speaking of this kind of people when he says:

> ... **be ye doers of the word, and not hearers only, deceiving your own selves.**
> **James 1:22**

A Common Misconception

It seems as if there is some flaw in the nature of Christians that causes them to think they automatically possess the benefits of a scripture by just hearing it. This assumption is absolutely untrue! The truth is the exact opposite, for in Christianity, it actually becomes a liability *to know a truth and not to act upon it.*

> ... to him that knoweth to do good, and
> doeth it not, to him it is sin.
> James 4:17

Faith Without Works

Miracles come to those who have the faith to receive them. We have seen in a previous chapter that the miracle of cancelled debt is real. We have also seen that it is readily available. However, like most of God's blessings, it is conditional. You must have living faith to receive it. Notice that when I say *faith,* I mean really strong faith. It takes more than just a wish. Once again, we must hear the Apostle James on this matter, for he tells us if we have not put action (works) with it, our faith is dead. Be assured that dead faith will not have the ability to draw the miracle of debt cancellation into your life.

> ... faith, if it does not have works (deeds
> and actions of obedience to back it up), by itself
> is destitute of power (inoperative, dead).
> James 2:17, Amplified

The King James Version says it a bit more bluntly. It simply says, "Faith without works is dead." Faith alone cannot accomplish anything.

Stop Doing the Old Things

If you are going to enjoy God's debt-free guarantee, there are some basic things you are going to have to stop doing. You will have to *stop impulse buying.* It may take a rubber band around your checkbook, or better yet, a two-signature checking account so that your spouse or financial counselor can help you decide if the thing you are about to purchase is really necessary. You should have a readily available list of qualifications an item must meet before you will purchase it.*

You will also have to *give up credit cards* (unless you pay the balances in full each month). I like to refer to this process as "plastic surgery." You will have to take the scissors to your plastic credit cards and do some surgery on them.

You must immediately *close any open charge accounts.* (These accounts exist primarily in smaller towns where the local hardware or grocery store or gas station allows trusted customers just to sign for their purchases.)

Immediately *remove* any and all *easy-purchase, pay-later systems* that may have attached themselves to you before you decided to become debt free. Make it a hard and fast rule to pay for whatever you purchase as soon as you receive the goods or services. No more *lay-away plans* either. As rough as it may seem, it is best if you just go *cold turkey* and stop spending for anything except the necessities of life.

Please take note that the Bible does not teach a no-luxury lifestyle. However, if it is your heart's desire, getting out of debt will call for a new resolve on your part.

---

*   *To receive "Questions to Ask Yourself Before Going Into Debt," write to the address at the back of this book and request your free copy.*

You will have to go through a season of belt-tightening while you are paying off the deficit spending of the past.

Keep in mind that people who succeed in living in God's debt-free guarantee have made a quality decision to stop going into debt. They have made up their minds they are *getting out of debt*. They concentrate on using every spare cent they can get their hands on to pay off their existing bills. They become *fanatically committed* to not going any further into debt.

> *Testimony:*
> We implemented the strategies that you outlined in your books and tapes, and God has blessed us. Just within the past two years, the Lord has delivered us from approximately $400,000 of debt. *E.W.—Kenner, LA*

The Debt-Free Language

You must do a second thing if you want to bring the full power of stone #2 into your out-of-debt program. *You must start speaking* as if you are going to get out of debt. Let me illustrate.

Many years ago I met a man named Ike Gabbert. He was a Cumberland Presbyterian preacher who lived in the outback of Kentucky. When I say *outback,* I mean really primitive, rural Kentucky. Each afternoon, I would visit with him on his front porch, and he would teach me wonderful truths about God from his old, worn Bible.

During those front-porch sessions, neighbors would often stop by. Each time the old preacher would see a neighbor approaching, he would make the same statement. I can still hear him as he would say, "Here comes a person who says he is going to heaven. Let's see if he has anything to say about heaven."

After several of these visits I asked, "Why do you always make that same statement about your neighbors?" Pastor Gabbert looked at me and said, "John, I have found that people will always *talk about the place they are going.*"

What a wonderful truth that old, circuit-riding preacher dropped into my spirit! It is powerful because it's a Bible truth. Please see if the following verse doesn't say almost the same thing.

> **For verily I say unto you, That whosoever shall say unto this mountain, Be thou removed, and be thou cast into the sea; and shall not doubt in his heart, but shall believe that those things which he saith shall come to pass; *he shall have whatsoever he saith.***
>
> **Mark 11:23**

Talk About It

Yes, it's a fact. *People do talk about where they are going.* If you notice, people going on vacation talk about the places they will visit. People about to get married will be talking about their wedding. A family about to move to another part of the country will have much to say about their new city.

Confession Works

If you really want to put another measure of biblical power behind your out-of-debt program, start talking about the debt-free life you are headed toward. Boldly begin to say, "We will soon be debt free." You should start saying, "We will not take thirty years to pay off our mortgage. Our plan is to have it paid in full in six years." Go right ahead and boldly say, "The automobile we are now driving will be the last one we will ever buy on time payments. Our next car will be a new one, and we will be paying for it with cash."

When you begin to state your intention of becoming debt free, it will do two definite things for you. You will be establishing a spiritual principle that will put the energy of God's Word to work in your out-of-debt plan (Mark 11:23). Not only that, but you will also receive the constant, personal fortification that comes from hearing your heart's desire (being out of debt) spoken out loud.

The Scriptural Principle

Please notice carefully that it takes more than just wishful words to operate the biblical principle of positive confession. Just constantly saying "I am going to be debt free" will not bring about a debt-free life. The Bible says you must also *believe the thing you are saying will come to pass.*

> ... whosoever shall say unto this mountain,
> Be thou removed, and be thou cast into the sea;
> and *shall not doubt in his heart, but shall believe*

> *that those things which he saith shall come to pass;*
> **he shall have whatsoever he saith.**
> **Mark 11:23**

Remember, it's not just talking that will add the extra power to accomplish your goal. Extra power comes only *when you believe the thing you are saying will actually come to pass.* When I say *believe,* I mean having the kind of faith that refuses to doubt that the things you are saying will become a reality.

Scripture tells us the words we speak and firmly believe are powerful. These faith-filled words are so strong they can bring forth life or death.

> **Death and life are in the power of the tongue. . . .**
> **Proverbs 18:21**

Just think about it. Your Bible says the faith-filled words you speak about your debt will cause it either *to live or to die.* I am simply saying that if you constantly speak of the overwhelming size of your debt, and how impossible it will be to overcome, your words will cause your debt to loom high above you. With each negative word, your debt will grow more impossible to overcome. However, if you constantly speak of your debt's becoming smaller, if your conversation emphasizes how much stronger God's power is than your debt, it won't be long until *you will see your debt begin to wither* and grow smaller.

This dynamic Bible truth will divinely energize your out-of-debt program. Your new attitude will work *for* you instead of *against* you. Start this very day to speak words of death to your debt, and words of life to your out-of-debt program.

Testimony:
We have had our first debt cancellation
We are expecting others! *J.B.—Wheaton, IL*

The Practical Application

A powerful truth exists in the world of sports called the "home-court advantage." Here is how it works. When he performs in his own hometown, an athlete is usually much harder to defeat than when he competes in a strange city. However, if his hometown fans boo and jeer him, if they talk only about his weaknesses and failures, the home-court advantage quickly becomes the *home-court disadvantage.*

For just a moment let's pretend you are an athlete. Let's say you are a wrestler and your name is Christian. Let's just imagine that your opponent's name is Debt.

If you wrestle for the championship in your hometown, how will the match go if all you hear from the hometown fans are cheers for your opponent? "Rah, rah, Debt! Go, Debt, go! Defeat Christian!" It doesn't take a genius to know there will be no home-court advantage if you hear everyone cheering for your opponent. Debt will gain the advantage, and he will probably have his way with you.

Now let's turn this situation around. Let's say the hometown fans are all cheering for you. They are booing Debt and making fun of him. Hear them as they give old

Debt the raspberries. "Debt is dead! Debt is dead! Christian is strong! Go, Christian, go! Whip Debt!" Psychologically, you would receive strength from the positive words you would be hearing. The exact opposite would be true for your opponent. He would become weaker because of the negative words he would be hearing.

This is a second advantage that comes from boldly speaking of your victory over debt. *You weaken the grip of debt* a bit more each time you speak of the day you will overthrow it.

On the other hand, if you are not careful, your words will continue to snare you. Better said, your words will actually strengthen the grip of debt on your life. With these thoughts in mind, notice how strong the Word of God is when it speaks of the power of words.

> **Thou art snared with the words of thy mouth, thou art taken with the words of thy mouth.**
> **Proverbs 6:2**

Confession Reveals the Heart's Desire

Strange as it may seem, you will not be totally committed to getting out of debt — I mean spirit, soul, and body — until you are able spontaneously to speak words about getting out of debt. Please notice, very few folks know the statement you are about to read. Let me word it carefully so that it can become a truth to you: *Until you start speaking spontaneously of being debt free, the words won't be coming from your heart.* Don't take my word for it. Hear God's own Word on the subject.

> **. . . out of the abundance of the heart the
> mouth speaketh.**
> **Matthew 12:34**

Hear it now from the Amplified Bible.

> **. . . For out of the fullness (the overflow, the
> superabundance) of the heart the mouth speaks.**
> **Matthew 12:34, Amplified**

It will be easy to speak about being debt free when you believe it with your whole heart.

Testimony Is Powerful

I want you to read just one more scripture on the power of God that will come to you from hearing your own voice speak words about being debt free. Everyone knows it is the devil's desire to overcome every Christian. He uses every possible trick to keep the children of God from spreading the gospel. There can be no doubt about it. The devil uses debt *to redirect much of the money the Church needs to evangelize the world* into monthly payments to the world system.

The Word of God plainly states that *you can overcome the plan of the devil* (debt) by repeatedly speaking of your soon-coming victory over debt.

> **. . . they overcame him by the . . . word of
> their testimony. . . .**
> **Revelation 12:11**

When you speak about your victories over any of the devil's opposition, you will strengthen yourself as well as those who hear you.

Testimony:

After sowing seed in your ministry and reading your books, we cancelled $18,000 of debts in one year. We know the remaining debts we have are already gone! *C. & D.B.— Hampton, VA*

You Won't Like It at First

Please don't let me disillusion you. You probably won't like getting out of debt at first. Eating at home instead of eating out, sacking your lunch, and carrying your coffee to work in a thermos bottle won't seem like fun things to do in the beginning. You may not like finding things to do around the house instead of riding around all weekend, burning up gasoline, eating hamburgers, and drinking soda pop. However, just give the plan a little time. When I say time, I mean at least enough time for you to pay off your first bill ahead of time. As soon as you have paid it, the whole process becomes fun.

Gang Up on Your Debts

From that point on, life will just keep getting better and better. As soon as you pay off the first bill ahead of time, immediately add the whole amount of that payment to the early payoff of the next bill. Suppose the first bill you pay off is a credit card with a $30 per month payment. When you apply that $30 payment to a department store bill with a $60 payment, you will then begin to make one-and-a-half payments per month on the department store bill. If it is scheduled to be paid off in nine months, your new payment-and-a-half will actually pay it off in six months. Why, that will be three months earlier than the devil had planned. Then the fun really begins, for now you have an extra $90 ($30 from the first bill and $60 from the bill you just paid off) to add to the payment of the next bill.

If the next bill also has a $60 per month payment, you will now be paying $150 per month on it ($90 + $60 = $150). This new amount will make two-and-a-half payments each month on the next bill. As you can see, at this rate you will be paying off the payments for a whole year in only five months. It won't take long for the *no fun* of getting out of debt, to become *the fun* of getting *rapidly* out of debt.

Power Rushes In

By talking about your soon-coming victory and working at paying off your debts, you are well on your way to the debt-free lifestyle. With your new determination to stop doing the things that got you into debt, and your absolute resolve to do only the things that will help get you out of debt, you will immediately feel the very life of God begin to flow into your out-of-debt program. You will have done exactly what God's Word prescribes. *You will have added the necessary works to your faith* and thereby assured that your faith will stay alive.

> . . . faith without works is dead.
> **James 2:20**

Remember, the Bible says that not only will your works keep your faith alive, but also your faith-filled confession will bring to pass the things you are speaking.

... whosoever shall say unto this mountain, Be thou removed, and be thou cast into the sea; and shall not doubt in his heart, but shall believe that those things which he saith shall come to pass; he shall have whatsoever he saith.

Mark 11:23

4

An Open Heaven

. . . I will . . . open you the windows of
heaven. . . .

Malachi 3:10

The powerful tool I will be placing in your hand in this
chapter is probably the easiest of the five stones to set in
motion, for it takes no more effort than just saying yes to
God's command. However, for some strange reason it is
missing from the lives of most Christians. *Please note that
this stone will not be optional in your war on debt.* It is
absolutely necessary if you want to live in God's debt-free
guarantee. You must operate your out-of-debt program
under an open heaven.

Good Things Come From Heaven

Every good thing you can possibly hope for has to
come to you from heaven. Your Heavenly Father, who is
the giver of all good things, is in heaven (Matthew 5:45).
All your durable treasures, if you have any, are laid up for
you in heaven (Matthew 6:20). Your guardian angel
watches over you from heaven (Matthew 18:10). When
God sends angels, they come to you from heaven (Luke
22:43). When He speaks to you, God speaks from heaven
(John 12:28). Spiritual visions come to you from heaven
(Acts 26:19). Why, everything that makes your
Christianity valuable comes from heaven.

The Miracle of Debt Cancellation Comes From Heaven

Every miracle of debt cancellation you read about in Scripture came from heaven. The widow with the multiplying oil had to have an open heaven for God to set her free from debt. Hers was a creative miracle, and there is only one Creator, and He lives in heaven.

> **All things were made by him; and without him was not any thing made that was made.**
> **John 1:3**

The miracle of the borrowed ax head that swam could not have taken place without an open heaven. It is a scientific fact that iron cannot swim. However, there is One who can make iron swim, and He lives in heaven. He is God, and with Him nothing is impossible!

> **. . . with God all things are possible.**
> **Mark 10:27**

The miracle of debt cancellation for Nehemiah and his people took place under an open heaven. No lender in his right mind would ever release the debt of an entire nation without the intervention of heaven.

> **The king's heart is in the hand of the Lord, as the rivers of water: *he turneth it whithersoever he will.***
> **Proverbs 21:1**

When our Lord and Savior Jesus Christ experienced the miraculous debt cancellation with the money in the fish's mouth, His miracle most surely came through an open heaven, for Jesus walked simultaneously *in heaven* and *in earth.*

> ... no man hath ascended up to heaven, but he that came down from heaven, even the Son of man which is in heaven
>
> **John 3:13**

You must now make a quality decision, for if you hope to walk in God's debt-free guarantee, you must walk under an open heaven. You must be an *uncompromising tither.*

Testimony:
Since I have been consistent in my tithes and offerings, doors have started to open up for me as well as pay raises. This is truly a miracle of debt cancellation. *J.B.—Los Angeles,* **CA**

Tithing Opens Heaven

It takes only a brief look at Scripture to realize you must be a tither if you hope to have an open heaven.

> Bring ye all the tithes into the storehouse, that there may be meat in mine house, and prove me now herewith, saith the Lord of hosts, *if I will not open you the windows of heaven....*
>
> **Malachi 3:10**

Tithes Are Paid, Not Given

Scripture clearly teaches that the tithe belongs totally to God. It is not the property of the person who pays it. It is the property of God. The person who pays it has only been entrusted with it for a short period of time.

> ... *all the tithe* of the land, whether of the seed of the land, or of the fruit of the tree, *is the Lord's:* it is holy unto the Lord.
> **Leviticus 27:30**

Notice that the writer of Hebrews does not refer to the act of tithing as giving tithes. He calls it *"paying tithes."*

> ... Levi ... paid tithes in Abraham.
> **Hebrews 7:9**

Also notice he doesn't say the Levites *received* the tithe. He says they *took* the tithe from the people.

> ... the sons of Levi ... *take tithes* of the people....
> **Hebrews 7:5**

Jesus Himself spoke of the tithe as being paid instead of being given.

> ... for ye pay tithe of mint and anise and cummin ... these ought ye to have done....
> **Matthew 23:23**

Not Tithing Is Stealing

If God's Word is clear about anything, it is that the person who doesn't tithe is actually stealing from God. God says the non-tither has robbed Him.

> Will a man rob God? Yet *ye have robbed me.* But ye say, Wherein have we robbed thee? In tithes and offerings.
> **Malachi 3:8**

Harsh Words

The words you just read may seem a bit strong. However, they come directly from the Holy Bible. You must keep in mind that just because our God is a good God doesn't mean He is not a just God. True justice usually calls for strong words.

A quick look at Scripture will reveal that the tithe is only one of many things about which God speaks strongly. He surely uses forceful language when He speaks of the eternal destiny of those who reject Christ. He says they will burn forever in hell (Revelation 20:15). He also uses harsh words when He gives His opinion about those who refuse to work or support their families. He says they should *not be allowed to eat* (1 Timothy 5:8; 2 Thessalonians 3:10).

Everyone who reads the Bible is aware that it is a book of strong language. God has to use stern words because He deals with fallen mankind about life-and-death issues. It only stands to reason that when He deals with something such as robbery, God must use strong language. It's not God's nature to be harsh, but the sin of robbing Him brings forth the harsh words. So please do not be offended with God about the forceful language He uses. Instead, be offended with the sin of not tithing which causes it.

Embezzlement

With this matter settled, I must now speak plainly about your responsibility to tithe. If you are not tithing, you are taking that which rightfully belongs to God and using it for yourself. It doesn't take a rocket scientist to know not tithing is a clear violation of God's commandments. In secular terms, not tithing is nothing short of embezzlement.

It's a Hard Way

Please know that anything you try to do as a non-tither becomes much more difficult to accomplish. For one thing, God will not extend His helping hand to you as long as you live under a closed heaven. If you will hear the following scripture with open ears, it will help you to understand that when you disobey (transgress) God's instructions, *everything in your life immediately becomes harder to accomplish.*

> ... the way of transgressors is hard.
> **Proverbs 13:15**

The Devourer

Not only does your way become harder, but not tithing looses into your life the spiritual entity the Bible calls *"the devourer."* Scripture shows only one way to stop the devourer from ruining every aspect of your life. The remedy is plain and simple. *You must immediately start tithing.*

> Bring ye all the tithes into the storehouse, that there may be meat in mine house, and prove me now herewith, saith the Lord of hosts, if I will not open you the windows of heaven, and pour you out a blessing, that there shall not be room enough to receive it.
> And *I [God] will rebuke the devourer for your sakes,* and he shall not destroy the fruits of your ground. ...
> **Malachi 3:10,11**

Your Timing Will Be Off

A second thing takes place under a closed heaven that will make your life harder. The timing of your entire life will be totally out of harmony with God's desire for you. Malachi tells us when you start tithing, God promises that *untimely events will stop* taking place in your life.

> . . . **neither shall your vine cast her fruit before the time in the field. . . .**
> **Malachi 3:11**

Upon close examination of Malachi 3:8-11, you will see that faithful tithing brings you an *open heaven* (verse 10). It will also cause God to *rebuke the devourer* for your sake. Finally, those *untimely, destructive events* that constantly spoil your ability to increase will stop happening (verse 11).

> **Thus saith the Lord, thy Redeemer, the Holy One of Israel; I am the Lord thy God which teacheth thee to profit, which leadeth thee by the way that thou shouldest go.**
> **Isaiah 48:17**

Testimony:
We have experienced a miraculous debt cancellation. We know why God has blessed us. We have never stopped giving our tithes and offerings as God designated. Even in the lean times, we were faithful stewards. *J. & L.E.—Birmingham, AL*

How to Tithe

While most Christians know how to tithe, it is still important that we take a moment and rehearse the mathematics of this important biblical principle. It is necessary to realize the tithe is not an optional amount of money. It is *a specific amount.* God's Word plainly states that the tithe is 10 percent of all the increase you receive.

> . . . all the tithe of the land, whether of the
> seed of the land, or of the fruit of the tree, is the
> Lord's: it is holy unto the Lord.
> **Leviticus 27:30**

It is quite easy to prove from God's Word that the tithe is *exactly 10 percent.* We can prove this percentage in two ways. First, the Hebrew word translated in the Bible as *tithe* literally means *"the tenth."* Another way of establishing beyond any shadow of a doubt that the tithe is exactly 10 percent is by comparing two verses of Scripture. They both speak of the same event: Melchizedek's meeting with Abraham.

Notice that in the Genesis account, the word the writer translated as *tithe* is describing the things Abraham gave to Melchizedek. When the Hebrews account uses it, the word *tenth* is speaking of those same things.

> . . . And he [Abraham] gave him
> [Melchizedek] *tithes* of all.
> **Genesis 14:20**

> Now consider how great this man
> [Melchizedek] was, unto whom even the
> patriarch Abraham gave *the tenth* of the spoils.
> **Hebrews 7:4**

This comparison should settle forever the question of how much the tithe is. It is not a discretionary dollar amount. It is a percentage (10 percent) of the total increase you receive.

Gross, Not Net

You should always figure the tithe on your gross income, not on your net income. God's Word tells us the tithe should be the firstfruits of your increase. Better said, it should be the first thing you pay from your increase.

> Honor the Lord with thy substance, and
> with the *firstfruits* of all thine increase:
> So shall thy barns be filled with plenty. . . .
> Proverbs 3:9,10

It should be clear from this scripture that you are to pay your tithe first. If you do not pay it first, you will not be honoring God with your firstfruits.

You should always allow your tithe to have preeminence over your taxes. Matthew 22:15-22 is proof of this rule. Here the Pharisees and Herodians asked Jesus whether or not God's people should pay taxes. Scripture tells us that the purpose behind their question was to trick our Lord into saying something they might use to accuse Him. If He said the people should pay taxes to Caesar, He would be in opposition to Jewish law. If He said not to pay Caesar's tax, He would be in opposition to Roman law. Verse 15 tells us they were trying to **". . . entangle him in his talk,"** or as we would say today, they were trying to trip Him up.

Notice how our Lord's answer kept everything in its proper order. After asking to see the coin, He asked whose face they saw inscribed on it. They said Caesar's. Then our Lord answered in a way that astonished them all.

> ... Render therefore unto Caesar the things which are Caesar's; and unto God the things that are God's.
> Matthew 22:21

Let me paraphrase His answer to clarify what He was actually saying. Jesus said, "Go ahead and give Caesar his tax. However, you must also give God that which is His (the firstfruits, or the tithe)." From this verse you can conclude that God and the government must both have their rightful places in your life. To give God His proper place, you must pay your tithe from your paycheck before you pay anything else. By paying it first, the tithe becomes your firstfruits. Then after you have paid the firstfruits to God, pay your taxes.

> *Testimony:*
> I am glad to report to you that all of our bills are paid except for the mortgage payment. God has blessed us abundantly! Our tithes and offerings now exceed my total income of seven years ago when we started tithing. *J.B.—Green Cove Springs, FL*

Where to Tithe

With only a few more words I will conclude the subject of how to gain an open heaven. Not only must you pay the tithe, but you must bring it to the proper place. In almost every case this place will be your *local church.* Thank God, good local churches are available to most Christians.

However, in rare cases they are not. For instance, you may be a shut-in, or you may live where a local church is not available. In these situations, you should find a ministry that will faithfully minister the Word of God to you on a regular basis. It might be a television network or a specific television or radio program. It might be a ministry that ministers to you by regular correspondence. With these circumstances in mind, let me re-emphasize that *whenever possible,* you should attend a good, local church and faithfully bring your tithes into that ministry.

Malachi 3:10 tells us to bring our tithe into the *storehouse of God* so that there may be meat in *His house.* By saying it this way, Malachi tells us the storehouse and God's house are one and the same place. Timothy gives us New Testament clarity on this subject by identifying the local church as the house of God.

> . . . know how thou oughtest to behave thyself *in the house of God,* which is *the church of the living God* . . . .
> 1 Timothy 3:15

Stone #3 Is Now Yours

You must now take firm hold of this powerful weapon, knowing that the open heaven belongs to those who faithfully tithe. If you are not a regular tither, you must now begin to tithe. In so doing, the energy of God will begin to flow freely against the devourer and against untimely events that keep you from prospering. When you have an open heaven, you have the third stone you will need to slay your Goliath of debt and to insure that God's debt-free guarantee will be yours.

> *Testimony:*
>   All I could do was cling to God's promise that if I was a tither and cheerful giver, He would open the heavens and pour out blessings upon me. Then I received a check for $20,000! I have just paid off my credit cards and purchased an automobile with cash. *L.Z.—Orlando, FL*

5

An Out-of-Debt Flow

Every informed child of God knows that forces flow through the spirit world. The Bible speaks about evil forces that war against the children of God in the heavenly realm.

> **For we wrestle not against flesh and blood, but against principalities, against powers, against the rulers of the darkness of this world, against spiritual wickedness in high places.**
>
> **Ephesians 6:12**

One of these powers of darkness is the *spirit of debt*.

Let me be quick to say there are also good forces that flow through the spirit world. These forces give us the upper hand in fighting the powers of darkness.

> **Now unto him that is able to do exceeding abundantly above all that we ask or think, according to the power that worketh [flows] in us.**
>
> **Ephesians 3:20**

The Golden Rule

Let's take a moment and study one of these good spiritual forces. It is the power that enforces *the golden rule*. Please notice that no one ever refers to the golden rule as the "golden good-idea," nor is it ever called "the golden suggestion." It is, in fact, the golden rule, or better said, it is *the golden law.*

Everything that truly operates as a law must have a power (force) behind it to enforce it. For instance, the law of gravity functions only when the power of gravity is present to enforce it. If you go beyond the influence of the power of gravity, the law of gravity immediately stops working.

It Always Works

The Word of God teaches us about a power that constantly enforces the golden rule. The Amplified Bible states it this way.

> . . . as you would like and desire that men would do to you, do exactly so to them.
> Give, and [gifts] will be given to you; good measure, pressed down, shaken together, and running over, will they pour into [the pouch formed by] the bosom [of your robe and used as a bag]. For with the measure you deal out [with the measure you use when you confer benefits on others], it will be measured back to you.
> **Luke 6:31,38 Amplified**

Add the following verses, and it becomes evident the golden rule is a perpetual law that God always enforces.

> For all the promises of God in him are yea, and in him Amen, unto the glory of God by us.
> **2 Corinthians 1:20**

> Every good gift and every perfect gift is from above, and cometh down from the Father of

lights, with whom is *no variableness, neither shadow of turning.*

James 1:17

It Works in Adverse Conditions

Notice the adverse circumstances in which our Lord tells us to test His golden law. He says to love your enemies, do good to those who hate you, bless those who curse you, turn the other cheek to those who slap you, and to whomever takes your cloak, also give him your coat.

The truth is that without a supernatural power to enforce it, the golden rule would not work. However, Jesus says *no matter how adverse the circumstances* may seem to be, whatever you want men to do for you, do the same to them.

You may well be asking if you can really depend upon this law to work. The answer is yes, you can, because a spiritual force backs it.

It Goes Against Natural Law

Anyone with an ounce of sense knows that in the natural realm, the above actions would not bring forth any benefit. When you love your enemies, bless those who curse you, or turn the other cheek to those who slap you, you are making a big mistake — that is, unless you know for certain that some force greater than human nature is ready to intervene and bring to pass the result God's Word promises.

Most high school students know a natural law that goes like this. "Every action causes an equal but opposite reaction." This law simply says if you give, you lose. If you have ten dollars and give away three of those dollars, you will not have thirty or sixty more dollars. You will, in fact, have only seven dollars left.

Now hold onto your hat. I am not rejecting scriptural truth. I am simply showing you that God's golden rule must have more behind it than just the desire of the one who uses it. As we will see in a moment, if it's going to work, it will have to have God's own power behind it.

Sowing and Reaping

The Bible tells us we will reap whatever we sow.

> **Be not deceived; God is not mocked: for whatsoever a man soweth, that shall he also reap.**
> **Galatians 6:7**

I can testify from experience that the law of sowing and reaping absolutely works. Please don't misunderstand. I am aware that in the natural realm, things do not increase, they decrease. However, things are different when it comes to sowing and reaping, because God has put *the law of reproduction into place.* It is a law He maintains and enforces by His own power.

Now I will admit it takes a while for the thing you have sown to manifest itself. Nevertheless, it always will, for whatever a man sows is exactly what he will reap. It's a biblical fact, and it operates because God enforces it!

> *Testimony:*
> My wife and I fervently attacked our debts and at the same time began to plant seed. We have now paid off all of our debts. We can't keep up with the blessings God in showering down upon us. *I. J.—Broken Arrow, OK*

The Force Behind the Law

If it weren't for a statement in the Book of Ephesians, proving that God is the force behind the golden law would be much harder. However, Ephesians 6:8 not only says that God is the power behind the law, but it also shows you how to put this law to work in your own out-of-debt program.

> **Knowing that whatsoever good thing any man doeth, *the same shall he receive of the Lord,* whether he be bond or free.**
> **Ephesians 6:8**

There it is in the clearest possible language. God openly declares He is the power who makes the golden rule operate. Whatever good thing you do for someone else, *God will do that same thing for you.* Now notice carefully, an angel or some natural force won't do it. *Jehovah God* is the one who will do that same thing for you.

Personalize the Promise

Let's give some special thought to this promise. According to the information in Ephesians 6:8, if you found someone who was sincere about becoming debt free — now I don't mean just anyone who said he wanted to be debt free, but someone who really wanted it as sincerely as you do — if you started helping that person to get out of debt, God would *have to* start helping you to get out of debt. There can be no question about this matter. If Ephesians 6:8 is true, and I know it is, if you start helping someone to get out of debt, God will no doubt look upon what you are doing as a good thing.

Now I want you once again to look at what the Word of God says will happen to you when you do a *good thing* for someone else.

> **Knowing that whatsoever *good thing* any man doeth, the same [thing] shall he receive of the Lord....**
> **Ephesians 6:8**

I'm sure you're getting it now! If you help someone each month with his out-of-debt program, you will receive from God the exact same thing you are causing to happen for him. Yes, you are hearing right. *God Himself will then help you get out of debt.*

Testimony:
We have been able to help others, and we have also been able to pay off completely the credit card debts we owed. *T.C.— Albuquerque, NM*

Limited Power Draws Unlimited Power

Now I don't know how much you may be able to do in helping someone else out of debt, especially if the restrictions of your own debt limit you. It doesn't matter, for the Word of God doesn't say if you do something really big for someone else, God will do the same for you. It simply says that *whatsoever good thing* you do for someone else, God will do that same thing for you.

Think of it. You can put God's *limitless out-of-debt power* to work for you. Just start putting some of your meager out-of-debt power to work for someone else.

Hook Up to the Force

Dear friend, I do hope you see the powerful force this action will bring to bear against your own debt. It will actually release the power of God against it. The limited force you exert in helping someone else out of debt *will unleash God's unlimited force to get you out of debt.*

The debt-free force I am encouraging you to release into your out-of-debt program is none other than the very power of God, and when you have that power working for you, the debt-free guarantee is easily within your grasp.

So, I have now placed the fourth stone into your hand. If you use it correctly, it will be a powerful weapon in your war on debt. In fact, it will be the very power of God made available to you. This weapon will give you the advantage you desire over the Goliath of debt that now holds you captive.

Testimony:

As a wedding gift from the lienholder of my car, we received the title free and clear with a card that read, "The Lord laid it upon my heart to release you from this debt so that you can become financially free in your marriage." This miracle came after we sowed into paying off the debt of our church. *N.S.— Jacksonville, FL*

6

Putting Heaven on Notice

... thy prayer is heard, and thine alms *are*
had in remembrance in the sight of God.
Acts 10:31

The fifth step in drawing the power of God into your
war on debt is extremely effective. Its action will focus
God's ongoing attention on getting you out of debt. We
have this promise on good authority, for an angel tells us
about it.

And he [the angel] said, Cornelius, your
prayer has been heard and harkened to, and
your donations to the poor have been known and
preserved before God [so that He heeds and is
about to help you].
Acts 10:31, Amplified

Angels Have Visited

Don't think it strange that an angel appeared to a man.
The Holy Bible records a number of angelic visitations.
Angels appeared to Abraham; an angel visited Jacob; an
angel even appeared to a donkey. An angel visited the
Virgin Mary. The night our Lord was born, angels spoke
to shepherds. Each of these events brought news from
heaven. However, the angelic visit Cornelius experienced
is special to our generation, for it reintroduces *a neglected
truth*. For many years the Church has been ignorant of this

69

truth. When we properly understand it, a powerful method of prayer once again becomes available to us.

The Visitation to Cornelius

The name Cornelius seems to appear from nowhere in the tenth chapter of Acts. While it is brief, this Gentile's appearance in Scripture is of the utmost importance, for his prayer catches the attention of God. The story of Cornelius seems insignificant compared to other Bible stories, that is, until you realize he is a Gentile. Until the events of the tenth chapter of Acts, the gospel has virtually not touched the entire Gentile world. However, when Cornelius mixes them together, his praying and bountiful giving become something more than praying or giving alone. The angel tells us the mixing of the two turns his prayer into a *memorial prayer.* Carefully notice that this special, *supercharged prayer* brings to Cornelius a *God-appointed visit* with the great Apostle Simon Peter.

> ... **Thy prayers and thine alms are come up**
> **for a memorial before God.**
> **Acts 10:4**

The angel goes on to tell us when Cornelius mixed his prayer with his giving, something else took place. Not only did God send the Apostle Peter to visit Cornelius, but He gave his prayer a place of prominence. God permanently suspended it in His sight.

> ... **Cornelius, thy prayer is heard, and**
> **thine alms *are had* in remembrance in the sight**
> **of God.**
> **Acts 10:31**

The Amplified Bible brings forth this truth more clearly. It shows that when we mix them together, praying and giving are perpetually suspended before God.

> ... Cornelius, your prayer has been heard and harkened to, and your donations to the poor have been known and *preserved before God* [so that He heeds and is about to help you].
>
> Acts 10:31, Amplified

Testimony:

I had got behind in my car payments, so I sent in two payments. In the meantime, I sowed a memorial prayer seed. Two weeks later, I got a get well card from the man who sold me the car. In the card was my check for the two payments torn in half. *V.A.— Indianapolis, IN*

God Honors Memorial Prayer

Notice that when we mix a proper prayer with generous giving, it becomes, as the Amplified Bible says, **"preserved before God [so that He ... is about to help you.]"** I can hear someone ask, "Brother John, this is the first time I have ever heard of mixing prayer with giving. Are you sure it's really okay to do it?"

Please know I am not suggesting you make a memorial prayer on the strength of only one mention of it in Scripture. In fact, in many instances in the Word of God, people just like you mixed their giving and praying for the purpose of drawing God's attention to their desires.

Hannah Added Giving to Her Praying

The Book of 1 Samuel tells about a godly woman named Hannah. She mixed her prayer with her gift and saw God's hand move almost immediately to fulfill her request. Hear her prayer.

> **And she vowed a vow, and said, O Lord of hosts, if thou wilt indeed look on the affliction of thine handmaid, and remember me, and not forget thine handmaid, but wilt give unto thine handmaid a man child, then I will give him unto the Lord all the days of his life, and there shall no razor come upon his head.**
>
> **1 Samuel 1:11**

Hannah's special prayer is for a child. Hear her heart's cry as she desperately asks God to remember her. Then observe closely as she *adds giving to her prayer.* She adds a gift of significant value, for she offers her firstborn son to God. Please notice that she makes this new prayer after years of asking and not receiving. However, when she adds giving to her praying, *only a few hours pass before God responds by granting her request.*

> **And they rose up in the morning early, and worshipped before the Lord, and returned, and came to their house to Ramah: and Elkanah knew Hannah his wife; *and the Lord remembered her.***
>
> **1 Samuel 1:19**

Testimony:
   I gave a memorial offering for my bills to be paid off and the salvation of my husband and two children. I have paid off all my bills, and my son is now saved.   My husband is coming soon. *L.E.—Lewisville, TX*

Jephthah Mixed Prayer and Giving

The Book of Judges tells us about Jephthah. God had asked him to lead Israel against the nation of Ammon. Scripture tells us about a crisis he faced at the height of the battle. When Jephthah called on them, the tribe of Ephraim refused to come to his aid.

> **And Jephthah said unto them [Ephraim], I and my people were at great strife with the children of Ammon; and when I called you, *ye delivered me not out of their hands.***
> **Judges 12:2**

Ephraim's refusal to help in the battle drastically shifts the balance of power against the army of God. Because of this power shift, Jephthah must pray a prayer that will receive an *immediate* answer. If God delays, all will be lost. How will he pray? What will he do to assure quick action from God? Notice that he chooses to approach God by adding giving to his praying.

> **And Jephthah vowed a vow unto the Lord, and said, If thou shalt without fail deliver the children of Ammon into mine hands,**
> **Then it shall be, that *whatsoever cometh forth of the doors of my house to meet me, when I return***

> *in peace from the children of Ammon, shall surely
> be the Lord's,* **and** *I will offer* **it up.** ....
> **Judges 11:30,31**

His request was simple. "Lord, deliver the children of Ammon into my hands." Then he supercharged the prayer by adding giving to it. *"Whatever comes out of my house first is yours, Lord."* Well, here is the most important question to ask about Jephthah's prayer. Was it effective? Did it speedily bring God's help to Jephthah? The answer is yes, it most certainly did.

> **So Jephthah passed over unto the children
> of Ammon to fight against them;** *and the Lord
> delivered them into his hands.*
> **Judges 11:32**

Testimony:
    I gave a memorial promise of $1,000 because we had a lot of debt that weighed so heavily on us. Then a $13,000 debt was paid off with money that we were not expecting to have. *G.H.—Bradenton, FL*

A Widow Mixes Her Giving and Praying

The story of one of the best-known widows who ever lived appears in the seventeenth chapter of 1 Kings. It is the story of a woman who saves her son's life as well as her own. She does it by adding giving to her praying. The Word of God tells us God asked her to perform a special task for Him. She was to take care of His choice prophet, Elijah.

**. . . I have commanded a widow woman
there to sustain thee.**
1 Kings 17:9

When Elijah arrives at the widow's house, something
is definitely wrong, for she refuses to feed him. Her reason
for refusing the prophet's request is that she is down to her
last meal, and there just won't be enough.

**. . . I have not a cake, but an handful of
meal in a barrel, and a little oil in a cruse: and,
behold, I am gathering two sticks, that I may go
in and dress it for me and my son, that we may
eat it, and die.**
1 Kings 17:12

A Woman of Prayer

Needless to say, this dear woman has been praying
about her dwindling supply of food for a long time. We
know she is a godly woman, and therefore a woman of
prayer. Surely God would not ask a woman who didn't pray
to take on such an important responsibility as caring for
His choice prophet.

We can also be sure she has been regularly praying
over her food supply, for she is a single mother. If single
mothers pray about anything, it is food. So we know she
has, no doubt, prayed again and again over her dwindling
supply of food. However, in spite of her prayers, the barrel
of meal and cruse of oil continue to decrease each day until
she is brought face to face with the death angel. Thank
God, Elijah is able to persuade her *to add some giving to
her prayers.*

> And Elijah said unto her, . . . make me thereof a little cake first, and bring it unto me. . . .
>
> And she went and did according to the saying of Elijah: and she, and he, and her house, did eat many days.
>
> And the barrel of meal wasted not, neither did the cruse of oil fail, according to the word of the Lord, which he spake by Elijah.
>
> 1 Kings 17:13,15,16

Testimony:

My daughters and I were several thousand dollars in debt. We made a memorial offering to the Lord through your ministry. In less than a year, God supernaturally paid off all but the school loans. *A.F.— Indianapolis, IN*

Jewish Leaders Mix Giving and Praying

This next illustration is one of the most important I have found in Scripture, for it moves Jesus to make an exception to the predetermined plan. It causes Him to minister to a Gentile before the appointed day of the Gentiles has fully come (Acts 10).

The Book of Luke tells us about this man. He was the centurion who sent a request for healing to Jesus. He wanted the Lord to heal his favorite servant.

Keep in mind that the centurion is a Gentile, so he is not as yet qualified to receive the ministry of Jesus.

> . . . I am not sent but unto the lost sheep of
> the house of Israel.
> . . . It is not meet to take the children's
> bread, and to cast it to dogs [Gentiles].
> Matthew 15:24,26

These scriptures clearly show that the time of the Gentiles has not yet come. However, when they approach our Lord with the centurion's prayer for healing, the leaders of the Jews do something very powerful. They ask Jesus to grant his request because he (the centurion) is worthy. Then they purposely mix his request with his generous offerings.

> And a certain centurion's servant, who was
> dear unto him, was sick, and ready to die.
> And when he heard of Jesus, he sent unto
> him the elders of the Jews, beseeching him that
> he would come and heal his servant.
> And when they came to Jesus, they besought
> him *instantly, saying,* That he [the centurion] was
> worthy for whom he should do this:
> For he loveth our nation, and *he hath built*
> *us a synagogue.*
> Then [after He heard about his giving]
> Jesus went with them. . . .
> Luke 7:2-6

Hear the fifth verse again. However, this time hear it as the Amplified Bible puts it.

> For he loves our nation and he built us our
> synagogue [at his own expense].
> Luke 7:5, Amplified

This translation emphasizes that the centurion had used his own money to build the synagogue.

It is evident from this passage of Scripture that the priests of that day knew something about prayer that has been lost to our day. They knew that when someone mixes prayer with giving, it becomes much more persuasive. Therefore they mixed the centurion's prayer with his giving, making it into a memorial prayer. Did it work? The Bible says it did, for Jesus went with the leaders and healed the centurion's servant.

A number of other accounts in Scripture tell us about mixing praying and giving together. In each of these instances, the same result occurs. *God quickly moves to assist the person* who has formed his prayer in this way.

Testimony:
   Our seven-year-old daughter had emergency surgery. We were without insurance and had no means to pay the $20,000 bill. We sent you $1,000 and asked you to pray. Before long we received notice that everything was paid in full, and we did not have to pay one cent. M.M.—*Santa Margarita, CA*

Suspend Your Prayer in God's Sight

It is now time for you to take this most powerful step in your war on debt. You must permanently position your out-of-debt petition before the throne of God.

Notice again that when Cornelius mixed his giving and praying together, two things happened. Cornelius *permanently suspended* his prayer before God. He also received assurance that God was ready to help him.

> . . . Cornelius, your prayer has been heard
> and harkened to, and your donations to the poor
> have been known and preserved before God [so
> that He heeds and is about to help you].
> **Acts 10:31, Amplified**

In the next chapter I will help you launch your own war on debt. I will assist you in putting all five of these wonderful principles to work in your life.

7

Your Goliath Must Fall

In the preceding chapters, I introduced to you five strategies that will quickly take you out of debt. Each one comes with the promise of releasing a measure of God's power into your war on debt. Let's go over them one more time before putting them to work for you.

Stripped Naked by Goliath

In chapter one, you learned what debt really is. It is a Goliath that strips the captives and leaves them naked. It is a terror that most of the Church today faces.

You also learned that debt has the ability to turn you permanently into the servant of the financial system of the world.

> ... the borrower is servant to the lender.
> **Proverbs 22:7**

While most Christians know these things, it's sad that the vast majority of God's children are caught hopelessly in the relentless clutches of debt.

Recruiting God's Power

In chapter two, you saw the first of five steps that will draw God's power into your personal out-of-debt program. It consisted of three things you must know, things that cause you to receive power from God that will help you out of debt. First, you must know God is a debt-cancelling God. To prove that He is, I clearly documented this fact by many scriptural accounts of people just like you whom God has miraculously set free of debt.

You saw a widow and her two sons receive a miraculous multiplication of oil that brought them out of the bondage of debt. You also saw a borrowed ax sink to the bottom of the river. Then upon the word of the man of God, it swam to the surface. You also saw a whole nation miraculously set free from all its debt in a single day. Best of all, you saw Jesus settle a tax debt with money that came out of a fish's mouth. Then you saw the slave Onesimus released from debt by a word from the Apostle Paul. You also saw divine debt cancellation during the 1650 years of the Mosaic law. Every seventh year was a year of release when creditors cancelled every debt. Every fiftieth year Israel celebrated the great jubilee as the creditors released all debts and returned all property.

You also learned that when you add Hebrews 13:8, **"Jesus Christ the same yesterday, and to day, and for ever,"** to the fact that God has cancelled debt before, this combination of truth brings even more of God's power to you. *If God cancelled debt before, you know He will do it again.*

You received another powerful piece of information in chapter two. You found that *your God is no respecter of persons.*

> . . . Of a truth I perceive that God is no respecter of persons.
> Acts 10:34

82

From this scripture you know God doesn't prefer Hannah, Jephthah, or the widow at Zarephath over you. The biblical conclusion you must draw from these passages is that *if He cancelled debts for others, He will do it for you.*

Now, please don't let my statement about a biblical conclusion throw you. The Word of God clearly states that the saints were to be examples to us.

Now all these things happened unto them for ensamples [examples]. . . .
1 Corinthians 10:11

God assures you that if He cancelled debts for others, He will surely cancel debt for you.

> *Testimony:*
> **We have had two miracles of debt cancellation, one for $8,000.** *M.B.—El Paso, TX*

In chapter two you also gained the knowledge that God wants you to be debt free. You saw this truth in Deuteronomy 28 where you read that the obedient child of God lends and does not borrow. With this knowledge, you can expect to receive inner strength from God. The reason is that *His callings are always accompanied by His enabling.* You now know if He wants you to be debt free, God will also give you the power to become debt free. Now hear this powerful verse once again, and remember it.

> **For with God nothing is ever impossible
> and *no word from God shall be without power or
> impossible of fulfillment.***
> **Luke 1:37, Amplified**

This verse tells you that the very Word of God which revealed to you that He wanted you to be debt free, also contains within it sufficient power to accomplish this desire. If God's Word says He wants you out of debt (Deuteronomy 28), God's power will come with His Word to get you out of debt (Mark 1:27).

Faith That Works Is Alive and Well

In chapter three you learned two important things you must start doing. They will bring even more of God's power into your out-of-debt program. There is no way to get around it. *People who get out of debt do certain things.* They stop deficit spending. They stop recklessly wasting their money. They focus their energy on paying off their bills. By mentioning just these few things, it becomes obvious that in coupling your faith in God to get you out of debt, with the works that go along with getting out of debt, something has to happen. For one thing, the faith it takes to succeed will not die. It will continue to be vibrant, living faith, the kind of faith that will see you through to victory.

> **. . . faith, if it hath not works, is dead, being
> alone.**
> **James 2:17**

You also learned another thing you must begin doing. You must begin to speak as if you are getting out of debt. I usually put it this way. You will have to start talking *the out-of-debt talk.* You must begin to make bold, out-of-debt statements such as, "This is the last automobile I will ever buy on time payments." "Under no circumstances will it take thirty years to pay off my home." "As for me and my house, we choose to be debt free."

Not only did you realize that speaking as if you are becoming debt free psychologically strengthens you, but if you speak in faith believing, God will cause the things you are saying to come to pass.

> . . . Have faith in God [have the God-kind of faith].
> For verily I say unto you, That whosoever shall say unto this mountain, Be thou removed, and be thou cast into the sea; and shall not doubt in his heart, but shall believe that those things which he saith shall come to pass; he [you] shall have whatsoever he saith.
> Mark 11:22,23

Faithfully doing the things you learned in chapter three will bring even more of God's power into your out-of-debt program.

Testimony:
I have read your books and am using [their principles]. To my amazement, I will have this house paid for in only a few years.
J.B.—Brownwood, TX

Heaven Must Be Open

Chapter four spoke to you about something most Christians know God requires, but few ever do. There you saw that the miracle of debt cancellation, as well as any other help the Lord might want to give you, must come through the open windows of heaven. You know from Scripture that an open heaven exists only over those who tithe.

> **Bring ye all the tithe into the storehouse, that there may be meat in mine house, and prove me now herewith, saith the Lord of hosts, if I will not open you the windows of heaven....**
> **Malachi 3:10**

You also saw that when you tithe, *God rebukes the devourer.* Better said, God renders the devourer powerless in the lives of those who faithfully tithe.

> **And I will rebuke the devourer for your sakes....**
> **Malachi 3:11**

With the windows of heaven open and the devourer of your goods soundly rebuked and disarmed, the miracle of debt cancellation becomes much easier to receive. God can now reach through the open heaven your tithe has produced and pour out blessings beyond your wildest imagination.

Testimony:
The very day I made up my mind that no matter what, I was going to tithe, my husband was called back to work after being unemployed for seven months. *R.S.— Pembroke Pines, FL*

Create an Out-of-Debt Flow

Chapter five gave you the information you need for bringing even more of God's power into your out-of-debt program. It gave you a sound, biblical plan that guarantees God's assistance to those who properly follow it. The scriptural focus of this chapter contains one of God's most explicit promises. It promises to help you get out of debt if you will help someone else out of debt.

> **Knowing that whatsoever good thing any man doeth, the same shall he receive of the Lord, whether he be bond or free.**
> **Ephesians 6:8**

This verse could not be more plain. The Bible promises that when you help someone else with a good thing like getting out of debt, God will personally help you get out of debt.

Testimony:
We could barely afford to buy your book, but we also bought one for a single mom in our church. We have been able to pay off all our debts, and she [the single mom] became debt free and got off welfare!
B.S.—Jackson, CA

Strategically Positioning Your Petition

Chapter six introduced you to a long-neglected truth. In it you saw Hannah, Jephthah, the widow at Zarephath, the centurion, as well as Cornelius mix their most earnest desires (prayers) with their best gifts. You saw that this action immediately became special to God. You know this truth because one of His angels said the mixing together of praying and giving causes the prayer to become *a perpetual memorial before God.* The angel went on to say that when He sees it, *God is ready to answer the prayer quickly.*

> ... Cornelius, your prayer has been heard and harkened to, and your donations to the poor have been known and preserved before God [so that He heeds and is about to help you].
> Acts 10:31, Amplified

Making Your Memorial

To make your out-of-debt memorial prayer totally effective, you must mix your prayer with a proper offering, one that will suspend your request before the Father. You must search your heart and decide on an amount to give that will truly represent *your sincerity about getting out of debt.* When deciding on the amount, please remember, if the amount you give is *truly significant* to you, it will surely be *significant to God.* However, if it is insignificant to you, it will be insignificant to Him.

I have known this truth for a long time. *If it doesn't move me, my offering surely won't move God.* You see, God feels the same way about your offering as you do.

> For we have not an high priest which cannot be *touched with the feeling of our infirmities* [humanity]. ...
> Hebrews 4:15

The Amplified Bible says it this way:

> For we do not have a High Priest Who is
> unable to understand and sympathize and *have a
> shared feeling* with our weaknesses. . . .
> Hebrews 4:15, Amplified

Testimony:

    I didn't have the money to repair my car so I went to God in prayer and gave a memorial offering. I prayed for a miracle of debt cancellation, and within the month, the company I bought the car from cancelled the remainder of the debt and gave me the title free and clear. They also fixed everything wrong with the car. The car lot manager repeatedly said he didn't know why he was doing it. *L.B.—Columbus, OH*

As soon as you can say, "Yes, I believe, and I will put all five of these steps to work," you will be on your way to a total victory over debt. If you can say, "Yes, I believe, and I am ready to start," just complete the form on the next page and mail it to me at this address:

John Avanzini
P. O. Box 917001
Ft. Worth, TX 76117-9001

I eagerly await hearing from you so that I can take your memorial prayer before the Father and agree with you about getting out of debt as soon as possible.

My Declaration of Acceptance of God's Debt-Free Guarantee

I, _____, do hereby determine to put into action all five of these powerful, out-of-debt strategies.

- *Things I know:* My God cancels debt, He is no respecter of persons, and He wants me to be debt free.

- *Things I will do:* I will begin to work at getting out of debt and speak as if I am getting out of debt.

- *An open heaven:* As for me and my house, we will have an open heaven by faithfully tithing.

- *The golden rule:* I will help someone else out of debt, knowing that as I do, God will help me out of debt.

- *My memorial prayer:* I will mix my giving with my prayer to be debt free. I am giving a good and proper gift, one that demonstrates my sincerity. My gift will be $_____. This is a significant amount to me, and I know it will memorialize my prayer in God's sight.

Please print neatly.

Name:_____

Address:_____

City:_____State:_____Zip:_____

Area Code and Phone (_____)_____

Complete this form, enclose it in the envelope in the back of this book, and mail it today!

Books by John Avanzini

Always Abounding
Enter a new dimension of abundant living through a
plan from God's Word that cannot fail.   **$5.95**

The Debt Term-O-Nator
Focus on early payoff of mortgage and credit-card debt.
Edited from *Rapid Debt-Reduction Strategies*.   **$5.95**

Faith Extenders
Learn how you can use biblical methods of Abraham
and other Bible characters to increase your faith.   **$7.95**

Financial Excellence
This powerful treasury of wisdom is the result of many
years of Bible study and covers a number of dynamic
financial principles.   **$9.95**

Hundredfold
See clearly the scriptural laws of seed-time and harvest,
God's plan for your increase.   **$7.95**

It's Not Working, Brother John!
If you haven't manifested God's promises, find out how
you may be closing the windows of heaven over your
life.   **$8.95**

John Avanzini Answers Your Questions
Find the answers to the twenty most-often-asked
questions about biblical economics.   **$6.95**

Powerful Principles of Increase
Find out how you can take the resources of this world to establish God's Kingdom. **$8.95**

Stolen Property Returned
See how to identify the thief, take him to the heavenly courtroom, and recover what he has stolen. **$5.95**

The Wealth of the World
Find help to prepare for your part in the great end-time harvest of souls and wealth. **$6.95**

The Financial Freedom Series

War on Debt
Financial Freedom Series, Volume I — If you are caught in a web of debt, your situation is not hopeless. You can break the power of the spirit of debt. **$7.95**

Rapid Debt-Reduction Strategies
Financial Freedom Series, Volume II — Learn practical ways to pay off all your debts — mortgage included — in record time. **$12.95**

The Victory Book
Financial Freedom Series, Volume III — This workbook takes you step by step through The Master Plan for paying off every debt. **$14.95**

Have a Good Report
Financial Freedom Series, Volume IV — Find out what your credit report says about you, and learn the steps that will help you correct negative information. **$8.95**

**Complete both sides of this order form
and return it to HIS Publishing Co.
to receive a 10% discount
on your book order.**

Qty	Title	Cost	Total
	Always Abounding	5.95	
	The Debt-Free Guarantee	5.95	
	The Debt Term-O-Nator	5.95	
	Faith Extenders	7.95	
	Financial Excellence	9.95	
	Hundredfold	7.95	
	It's Not Working, Brother John!	8.95	
	John Avanzini Answers Questions	6.95	
	Powerful Principles of Increase	8.95	
	Stolen Property Returned	5.95	
	The Wealth of the World	6.95	
	War on Debt	7.95	
	Rapid Debt-Reduction Strategies	12.95	
	The Victory Book	14.95	
	Have a Good Report	8.95	
	Subtotal		
	Less 10% Discount		
	Shipping & Handling		2.00
	Total Enclosed		

(   ) Enclosed is my check or money order made
       payable to **HIS Publishing Company**

Please charge my: (   ) Visa   (   ) MasterCard

(   ) Discover   (   ) American Express

Account # ☐☐☐☐☐☐☐☐☐☐☐☐☐☐☐☐

Expiration Date _____ / _____ / _____

Signature_____

To assure prompt and accurate delivery of your order,
please take the time to print all information neatly.

Name_____

Address_____

City_____State_____Zip_____

Area Code & Phone (_____)_____

Send mail orders to:

HIS Publishing Company

P.O. Box 917001

Ft. Worth, TX 76117-9001